A Quive

Some Memoirs of a Prep School Head

by

Malcolm Innes

Illustrated by James Burgess

A John Catt Educational Publication

First Published 1999

by John Catt Educational Ltd,
Great Glemham, Saxmundham, Suffolk IP17 2DH
Tel: 01728 663666 Fax: 01728 663415
E-mail: enq@johncatt.co.uk
Internet: http://www.johncatt.com

Managing Director: Jonathan Evans Editor-in-Chief: Derek Bingham

ISBN: 0 901577 36 7

Set and designed
by John Catt Educational Limited

Printed and bound in Great Britain
by Bell and Bain Ltd, Glasgow, Scotland.

Like as the arrows in the hand of the giant:
Even so are the young children,
Happy is the man that hath his quiver full of them

Psalm 127

CONTENTS

PREFACE 7

FOREWORD 9

CHAPTER ONE

I do not ask to see the distant scene;
one step enough for me. 11

CHAPTER TWO

I trace the rainbow through the rain 19

CHAPTER THREE

No goblin nor foul fiend
Can daunt his spirit 25

CHAPTER FOUR

Oh happy servant he,
In such a posture found! 32

CHAPTER FIVE

Could we but climb where Moses stood,
and view the landscape o'er 37

CHAPTER SIX

In wisdom let us grow,
As years and strength are given 44

CHAPTER SEVEN

The lot is fallen unto me in a fair ground:
Yea I have a goodly heritage 51

PREFACE

This little book contains recollections and reminiscences from thirty five years of teaching in a boys' boarding Preparatory School. All the incidents described are true and as accurate as I can make them; I have never, however, kept a diary and have had to rely entirely on a not very good memory. I very much hope that I have not included anything that could hurt anyone's feelings; surnames therefore have been changed but the Christian names are, on the whole, correct.

I particularly want to thank James Burgess (a former pupil) for drawing the illustrations. He agreed to do so shortly before becoming engaged and, with commendable dedication, completed the drawings whilst on honeymoon. I would also like to thank Mark and Jane Maxwell-Hyslop; Mark for decifering my handwriting and Jane for typing the text from Mark's dictation. I want also to thank Sue Young for encouraging me to put pen to paper despite my doubts about doing so. Finally I would like to thank Rupert Godsal for agreeing to write the Foreword and for his help, support and friendship over a number of years as my Deputy Headmaster.

One of the great rewards of teaching is the opportunity it gives to pass on to a new generation a love of those things in life which have given one pleasure. In my case this would be a love of English Literature (and I include the Authorized Version of *The Bible* and *The Book of Common Prayer*), an appreciation of Nature (particularly trees and wild flowers), a knowledge of classical music and the pleasure to be had from playing games (especially court games). I cannot imagine any other way of life which would have been half so fascinating, absorbing and rewarding and I would like to dedicate this small book to all my former pupils.

Malcolm Innes, Newtown Common, April 1999

FOREWORD

I was fortunate enough to work with Malcolm Innes for nineteen years. There are many reasons why he should be considered one of the great Prep school headmasters, but two stand out above all others. He really knew his boys – he considered it a bad day if he did not see or speak to every boy, and it was always impressive just how much he knew about each and every one of his charges. Perhaps his greatest attribute, however, is his sense of humour, his ability to see, and to revel in, the funny side of Prep school life.

There is never the slightest hint of sarcasm or malice in his humour, just a gentle appreciation of the absurdities that abound in the close-knit community. I have hugely enjoyed reading the anecdotes and being reminded of the boys, staff and incidents that Malcolm describes so well. And, of course, each one triggers off further memories; hooting with laughter on the first tee at Saunton when an extravagant air-shot was firmly blamed on the post-lunch Kummel; bemoaning the fact that he had given up his beloved pipe - "It gave one something to do when a mother burst into tears"; or his inimitable rendition of 'Massa's in the Cold, Cold Ground'.

There's a danger, in these days of policies and inspections, of losing sight of what is really important in teaching – the people, and not the pieces of paper. It is good to be reminded of what makes the best Prep school master by someone who certainly fits that description.

Rupert Godsal, Kingsclere, April 1999

CHAPTER ONE

I do not ask to see the distant scene;
one step enough for me.

(No 298, *Hymns Ancient & Modern*)

I rang the bell for silence in the dining room in order to say grace before lunch on my first day as headmaster.

"For what we are about to receive", I began and paused when I noticed the boy on my right shift his position from one leg to another. Have I said something wrong? I thought, this is the beginning of the meal, isn't it, not the end? So I continued "may the Lord make us truly thankful". Then all was revealed, or at least all his breakfast was revealed, as the shifty boy on my right turned towards me and was sick all over my shoes.

That was the second pair of shoes I had written off already that day as things had not been uneventful earlier in the morning; a lot earlier, in fact, as I had been woken by the dogs, which slept under my bed, barking at five o'clock in the morning. Leaping out of bed and wondering where I was I realized that the front door bell was ringing which was, together with the dogs' contribution, enough noise to awaken the dead let alone a fox from his earth. It had clearly awoken some of the far from dead eight-year-olds in the four dormitories on the floor above my room, known as the 'private side' but where privacy was at a premium.

There was a taxi at the door with two boys who had arrived earlier at Heathrow from Singapore, full of beans and bounce and wanting breakfast with, disappointingly, no signs whatever of jet lag.

From that moment on began 18 years of headmastering, without a minute's relief, coping with the needs of 150 boys, aged eight to thirteen, the demands of their parents, the problems of approximately 18 teaching staff and the disputes of countless domestic helpers and caterers, administrative staff, maintenance men and groundsmen and, not least, the defects of the Victorian building's plumbing system.

I had survived breakfast that morning and taken morning prayers for the first time, light-footedly avoiding the banana skin of the spoonerism in line one of the first verse: 'Kinquering congs their titles take, From the foes they captive make' (No 191 *Hymns A & M*).

I had returned to my desk to a pile of more than 20 letters, mostly from parents seeing if they could squeeze extra concessions out of a new headmaster who was not yet sure of himself. I had dictated my first half dozen letters while wondering whether the school secretary was thinking that the school Governors had landed her with a complete illiterate as her new boss. It was a merciful relief when, at last, I picked up my briefcase and set off down the corridor to teach; here was something which I thought I knew how to do and where I would be comparatively safe.

It was not to be. My classroom was up a flight of stairs and looked out over the school drive which curved away in the distance round the trunk of an enormous Wellingtonia, a tree which seems to be a compulsory fixture at most Prep schools. Walking down the drive, still in his suit from the day before because 'he' had not been unpacked yet, and carrying his brief case, was an eight-year-old boy just starting his second term in the school and looking, for all the world, intent on catching the 9.35 to Waterloo before proceeding to some lucrative job in the City.

Abandoning my pupils I rushed down the stairs, shot along the corridor vaulting over suitcases and the usual beginning-of-term bric-a-brac, and made it safely to the private side where, with no time to delay, I reached for my car keys and catapulted through the front door. There in the drive was not my car; of course, I remembered, I had moved it to make room for all the cars belonging to parents of new boys who always came on the first day of their first term to the front door to deliver their sons. I was also rather ashamed of my car when alongside the parents' cars and so had left it out of sight down by the kitchen garden. This involved a sprint of some 70 yards before I was united with my car and in a position to begin the pursuit in earnest.

Charles, the absconding boy in question, had discovered that the second term is always worse than the first, despite what everyone had told him, and had decided on the sensible plan of rejoining his parents, who had brought him down from London the previous evening and had gone on to spend the weekend in their country house, which was not too far from the school. What Charles found particularly galling was that his sister, who was not yet going to boarding school, would be having an enjoyable couple of days in the country while he was dumped back at school.

When he saw me at the wheel of my car he ducked under a barbed wire fence into a field of horses which was particularly muddy. We carried on negotiations initially across this fence: "no", he would not get into my car unless I promised to drive him straight to his parents' house. "No" I would not promise that, but would take him back to the school in order to discuss things. In which case, he said, he would cut across the field where my car couldn't follow and continue on his way home. It was at this stage that my first pair of shoes that day had to be written off. After further extended negotiations in mid-field, surrounded by some decidedly interested horses, I brought off an agreement of which even the U N Secretary-General would have been proud. Charles would get into my car (so ruining the carpets with mud) and I would drive back to the school front door, but I had to concede that all further discussions must be carried on in the car.

I knew that if I went into the building, he would take off again so (as the hands of my watch moved inexorably towards lunch time when I would be required to take charge in the dining room), I was forced to wait in the car, my shoes covered in wet and glutinous mud. Someone must discover us out here, I thought rather optimistically. Eventually the large red front door opened only for a mop to be stuck out, shaken vigorously and withdrawn again. It was now less than two minutes to the start of lunch so I had to abandon the car, rush indoors, find the 'Dame', who was also having her first day in a new job, explain about Charles and hand her the problem, run upstairs, change my shoes and try to wash some of the signs of the morning's activities off my hands and face before arriving, out of breath and looking wind-swept at the moment where this chapter began.

"For what we are about to receive, may the Lord make us truly thankful," had been the grace that was always said in the past. I was to say it several thousand times in the future but however familiar I was with the words I had to be careful to get them right. The reason was that from time to time I had thought up my own variants to the wording, for instance: "For what we are about to receive, may God forgive the caterers or … may sauce Béarnaise be provided," although after a while I realised if I were to have any chance of success I must tone it down to "… may HP sauce be provided."

Care in saying the grace correctly had to be taken not because familiarity had bred contempt but because familiarity might have bred carelessness or lack of concentration resulting in one of the variants being said in error. Familiarity breeding contempt reminds me of an exchange I once overheard between a younger boy and his rather important dormitory captain named Bumford. Bumford was admonishing the cheeky younger boy for calling him by his nickname 'Buttocks'. This nickname was particularly appropriate not only because of Bumford's surname but also, as luck would have it, because of his shape. The younger boy replied that he had used the nickname because contempt had bred familiarity and anyway if anyone was 'cheeky' it was Bumford. He then ran for his life from his dormitory down to the surgery where he was safe under the watchful eye of the nursing sister. Eventually I could stand the strain of saying grace correctly no longer and changed it to a Latin one.

Boys sat on tables according to their ages in the dining room and moved round one place a day. Certain places were designated for piling plates or taking them to the central trolley or refilling the water jug. The places on either side of the masters at the ends of the tables were where you had to watch your manners, pass the salt and make conversation. The compensation was that you were first in line for second helpings. I discovered over the years that the seat occupied on the right of the headmaster was known to the boys as the 'hot seat' and it may well have been the fact that he was in the hot seat that caused the boy on my right to be sick over my second pair of shoes that first day of term.

One boy whom I remember well occupying the 'hot seat' was called Matthew. He was a large, strongly built boy but with a gentle nature and excellent manners. As soon as we sat down after grace had been said he would always say, "would you like a glass of water, sir?" to which I would always reply, "well, actually, I would prefer a gin and tonic." He would then say, "right sir" and pour me a glass of water. On the last day of the winter term we were having a full Christmas lunch and Matthew was in the hot seat. When he had said his usual opening line I replied "well, as we're having turkey today I think I would prefer a glass of dry

white wine." Matthew's jaw dropped and his smile vanished and I realised that I had not given the expected response so I quickly added, "but on second thoughts, I think I'll have a gin and tonic." "Right sir," said Matthew and he got up and walked out of the room returning a few moments later with a silver salver on which was a glass with ice and lemon in it, a miniature bottle of gin and a bottle of tonic. He then poured out my gin and tonic and I was relieved to see the big smile back on his face.

Food was served out by the master, mistress or matron at the ends of the table and then passed down to each boy. On one occasion when, as a great treat, each boy had a chicken drumstick with potato and cabbage on his plate, one young boy got up from his place and carried his plate back to the master serving out and said the immortal line: "Actually, Sir, I only eat the breast." The master, who was himself a good advertisement for regular square meals, was apoplectic; it would have made a wonderful Bateman cartoon. The boy subsequently went on to make his first million pounds by the age of 21.

The rest of my first day was not without further events. There was an argument in the kitchen where an extremely excited cook was brandishing a knife so the head caterer asked for my assistance. The main school boiler (recently serviced) went wrong so that there was no hot water for showers after football in the afternoon. I noticed over the years that the boiler always broke down after being serviced, necessitating an expensive second visit from the firm in charge of the 14 different boilers in various school buildings. It reminded me of birthday parties when I was a child in Calcutta. The snake charmer would be booked to perform in the garden, blowing on his pipe while we all sat round to watch. When he had finished and we had all run off to some other excitement he would pack up to go but surreptitiously leave one snake behind in the plants of the herbaceous border. Next day when we scampered into the garden there would be six foot of snake hanging from a tree, watching our every move. Servants had to be sent to find the snake charmer, who was usually waiting outside the gates, to remove the snake at once which he was happy to do at considerable expense, and no doubt the snake was rewarded with a dead mouse or two for what had undoubtedly been a very convincing performance, meriting, these days, an Oscar for best supporting actor.

As the long first day drew to a close the thought of keeping up this pace for the whole term seemed daunting in the extreme. I decided to 'phone a friend who had been a headmaster for several years and asked him whether my experiences were normal in the life of a headmaster. "You'll find things get easier after the first year", was his comforting response.

CHAPTER TWO

I trace the rainbow through the rain

(No 359, *Hymns Ancient & Modern*)

Once I had realized that survival would have to be my main aim, rather than any distinguished period of headmastership in the annals of the school's history, it became necessary to adopt a more relaxed approach if my blood pressure was not to be regularly off the scale when checked by the school doctor. This, however, was not easy to achieve, especially as the demands of parents increased in line with the increase in school fees.

At this time allergies had become very fashionable and I was asked by the mother of an only and much treasured son to carry out an extraordinary mission. Charlie, who was a cheerful and likeable boy, apparently suffered from a variety of allergies (although I noticed over the years that most boys' allergies disappeared once the boys were back at school and covered with mud). If Charlie were to discover his mother's plan all would be to no avail as he would be very cross. Would I, therefore, when he was asleep, creep into his dormitory and cut a lock of his beautifully curly fair hair? This would then be sent by his mother to someone she had heard of in the West Country who would beaver away over this lock of hair thus effecting a cure to all Charlie's multifarious allergies.

Several attempts to carry out this dread deed had to be (in modern parlance) 'aborted' when Charlie showed signs of waking up. It then occurred to me, as I floundered around his dormitory in the dark with a torch in one hand (only to be used to accomplish the mission for fear of waking Charlie or indeed any of the other boys happily snoring in the room), and a large

pair of scissors in the other hand, with an envelope between my
teeth in which to place the lock, that some serious explaining of
an imaginative nature would be called for should Her Majesty's
Inspectors choose that moment to burst through the dormitory
door and flood the scene with electric light.

As regards allergies a list had to be compiled of what boys could or could not eat, wear or do. On one very cold afternoon the mother of twins 'phoned me up from many hundreds of miles away to say that on account of the extremely biting east wind her boys were not to play games that day. I said I would of course make a note of it and at that moment one of the twins ran past my study window wearing the skimpiest of shorts and a sleeveless vest while taking part in a cross country run.

Another boy, I was told in tones which suggested that I was not to query what she said, was allergic to all meat but could eat sausages. When I did question one case where the boy was said to be allergic to eggs by asking if that meant that he couldn't eat cakes or puddings, of which he was very fond, if they contained egg, the boy was whisked up to Harley Street to get a certificate signed by a specialist to say that the allergy to eggs applied in all cases but that cakes and puddings were exempt. One boy had to have all his clothes washed 'by hand with a special bland soap' for fear that otherwise he would be covered in a rash. My favourite allergy, however, involved a new boy called Hector who, after several days at school, was heard to say on the telephone to his mother: "Mummy, I'm allergic to this school."

Talking of specialists one boy named Robert, who was a delightful and friendly boy, was taken to see the eye specialist. "Now what's the particular problem?" he was asked. "Well, you see," he said confidentially, "I can't see the blackboard in 'G'." The specialist, not wishing to appear foolish nor wishing to seem to mistrust the boy, tried frantically to work out what 'ingee' was in schoolboy slang. It was some considerable time before the matter was resolved and it was discovered that 'G' was the name of the formroom where the light from the window reflected off the board to the exact spot where Robert used to sit.

Local names and colloquial phrases can cause complete chaos to those who are not aware of the correct connotation. On one occasion I was showing some 'prospective' parents round the school; 'prospective' in that they were possibly going to choose the school for their son rather than that the wife was pregnant (you see what I mean about the correct connotation). They were particularly keen to meet young James whom they knew well, so I asked a boy as we went round the school if he knew where James was only to receive the reply: "He's bird-watching in Spain." Spain was the boys' name for a wooded area in the school's grounds the shape of which on a map resembled Spain. My prospective parents were impressed at how seriously we took our hobbies and it seemed a pity to disabuse them.

On another occasion, when the choir was rehearsing with some visiting musicians before staging a concert locally, the choir master asked: "where's so-and-so?" A boy piped up promptly: "he's in the prison, sir." This caused some consternation among the lady musicians, who had heard that we were a tough school, and the clucking and tut-tutting had to be calmed by a lengthy explanation that 'the prison' was the boys' nickname for one of the sick-rooms with only one small window high up on the wall.

Local phrases and names became so much part of one's life that they can result in some bizarre thoughts especially when singing hymns in chapel each morning. I remember when I played left back in my Prep school first Xl that the right back, goal keeper and I would delight in bawling out the line: "And our defence is sure," from No 165 (*A & M*). The forwards responded with a raucous delivery of: "One the earnest looking forward" (No 292). Sadly we never sang No 509 which contains the line: 'By God, true Man, united' which would have brought the roof down because it was, at the time (as indeed it still is), many boys' favourite team.

Once a term we would practise the Common Entrance Examination for those who would be taking it in the near future. These practice exams were know as 'trials'. By chance on the morning concerned I selected hymn No 317 which contained the line: "Long as our fiery trials last". Only one boy's face lit up as realization dawned but it was a delight to behold. It is rumoured that many young children think the lines from No 344: "Can a woman's tender care Cease towards the child she bare?" are referring to a young female bear, but I think it must be apocryphal that a very small boy thought the line: "Gladly the cross I'd bear," referred to a cross-eyed teddy bear named "Gladly".

After the great storm of Thursday, 25th January 1990 we had five days with no electricity which meant that the organ would not work for the Sunday morning service in chapel. The temptation to include No 85, sung to accompaniment on the piano was almost overwhelming as it contains the line 'Be with thy church in saving power.' The boys had named the Sunday on the printed service sheet 'Power-cut Sunday'.

Many hymns need no special association in one's mind to bring a smile to one's lips. I have always wondered whether I could manage the line from No 277: 'With jasper glow thy bulwarks,' (particularly as I knew a dog called Jasper which knew exactly what to do with any bulwarks he came across), or the preposterous couplet from No 280 'The harpers I might hear, Harping on harps of gold'. I have mentioned earlier spending my childhood in India. The first available ship home after the war sailed from Bombay in 1945. We crossed the sub-continent from Calcutta and my mother, elder sister and I went aboard. My father, who was to remain in India, bid us farewell with the line from hymn No 358: 'Peace, perfect peace, with loved ones far away?' His delivery of this line however made clear that he was omitting the question mark.

A visiting preacher at a public school on one occasion failed to discover that the school's particular slang for 'trousers' was 'barns'. Unfortunately for him, but to the wild delight of 600 boys, he selected a verse from St Luke, chapter 12, as his text: 'What shall I do because I have no room where to bestow my fruits? And he said, This will I do: I will pull down my barns and build greater.' At a carol service I heard a rather nervous boy reading the lesson say: "Most highly-flavoured lady" and of course, once one has thought of it, it becomes almost impossible not to say it. I felt sorry for the boy because I know how easy it is to become confused. I had to make a rule never to drink any spirits before taking evening prayers at 8pm in case in the passage to be read I came across the line: 'Jesus of Nazareth passeth by.' I find it difficult enough to say even when sober. It was also after a carol service containing 'We three Kings of Orient are' that a small boy was genuinely puzzled and asked, "Please, Sir, where's Orienta?"

As a staff we regularly went to Harlech for a week every April to play golf at the Royal St David's course. Our group was joined by other (usually teaching) friends and on one occasion included Colin, a classical scholar and public school housemaster. The hotel we stayed at deteriorated year by year but afforded us some amusement until we finally had to move elsewhere. The wine waiter always found it necessary to hum loudly while opening the claret we had ordered, first shaking it vigorously, and one young waiter was so nervous at a large party of school masters that his hands shook while serving us. We called him 'Tremens' (not to his face) and were always trying to think of ways to give him his confidence. At dinner one evening he had a particularly violent bout of tremens and spilt a dish of vegetables garnished with parsley all over one of our party. "Ah," said Colin, "I've always wondered what that line in the hymn meant: 'with sudden greens and herbage crowned?' " (No 179). Subsequently I had the great good fortune to have Colin as my chairman of Governors for most of my time as headmaster which made Governors' meetings hilarious occasions to the envy of my fellow headmasters who for the most part dreaded them.

CHAPTER THREE

*No goblin nor foul fiend
Can daunt his spirit*

(No 293, *Hymns Ancient & Modern*)

The plumbing of the Victorian building certainly seemed to be inhabited by its quota of goblins. Airlocks were frequent and the bursar kept a length of rubber piping to hand with which he would dash off to sort out the problem. We returned after one particularly cold spell in the Christmas holidays to find all of the water pipes in the private side frozen. This meant that once the boys were back and occupying the top floor of my end of the building all the lavatories had to be flushed with buckets of water carried from more fortunate parts of the building hundreds of yards away where water still flowed. When the thaw finally came we found we had 26 burst pipes.

After several days of not being able to have a bath (something guaranteed to 'daunt my spirit' quicker than anything else) water finally came out of the taps and I rejoiced in the luxury of a steaming soak in my huge old-fashioned tub. On pulling out the plug, however, the water refused to make an exit down the pipe and the bath could only be emptied by my hanging from the boys' fire escape and pouring boiling water from the kettle on the point where the waste pipe emerged from the brickwork. I can sympathize with the psalmist who says: "My soul is vexed within me ... Because of the noise of the water pipes." (Psalm 42).

On one occasion when I was assistant housemaster in one of the houses across the playing fields I returned there for a bath after playing squash. As I closed the bathroom door and turned the key in the lock the key snapped in half. I was safely locked in but unable to unlock the door to get out. Deciding to have my

bath and to consider while bathing what to do, I went ahead
calmly. But gradually I realized that there was no solution; the
door opened inwards so could only be forced from the outside.
From the window I could see a lane through the school grounds
and I waved my bath towel frantically whenever I saw a member
of staff drive past, but to no avail. After an hour-and-a-half I
remembered that the boys would be coming over in half-an-hour
for baths and there I was locked in their bathroom. I also felt a
very strong desire for a gin and tonic and this moved me to
desperate thoughts. I opened the window and thought I could
drop down avoiding the dustbins outside the kitchen window
when, just at that moment, I heard the sound of the elderly
matron entering the kitchen. It then occurred to me that as I
dropped down past the kitchen window my silk dressing gown
would blow up over my head like an unopened parachute and
the elderly matron would get a distinctly unpleasant shock. So
that plan had to be abandoned. Eventually I jumped up and
down on the bathroom floor, spurred on by the thought that
release would bring that gin and tonic, until the bemused matron
came upstairs to investigate. I shouted through the locked door
and explained what had happened and asked her to send for the
bursar. Finally he arrived and, at the third attempt, charging with
his shoulder, managed to break the door down.

Goblins could be busily at work in all sorts of ways. On one
occasion I had asked a public school master to preach a sermon
at our Sunday service before looking round and meeting boys
entered for his school. As usual I asked if he would like any
particular hymns or lessons and he sent me the reference of a
lesson on which he would base his sermon. I put the reference
up on the staff common room board and one master volunteered
to read it. All went well until we came to the lesson concerned
which was the second lesson in the service. The master duly
fetched up at the lectern and then launched into a diatribe which

contained various outspoken strictures about adultery and fornication. I realized that something had gone badly wrong, particularly when I saw the visiting preacher grab for his notes and start trying to revise and reorganize his intended sermon. After the lesson the boys sang one of the canticles which was normally followed by the Creed, instead of which I set off for the lectern saying to the harassed-looking visiting preacher out of the side of my mouth as I passed him: "I'll now read your lesson." Years later he told me that he had dined out on the story many times and that it was the only service that he had ever attended where three lessons were read.

Every year there was an adult cricket match played at the school between a team mainly of our old boys and a distinguished cricket club founded by a well-known cricket correspondent. Our team was made up of our best players over the previous twenty or so years and contained some blues and the occasional county player. The opponents sometimes produced a former test match player much to the excitement of the boys. The parents would all come for the day with a picnic and cars would be parked all round the boundary with, from time to time, a windscreen receiving a direct hit (also to the boys' delight).

After the match was over I would entertain the cricketers and their wives to drinks in my garden. On one occasion the drinks party was interrupted by a woman who silenced everyone by announcing that something terrible had happened. Her handbag, picnic basket and car keys had been stolen. She said that she was a university professor who had recently been lecturing at St Andrew's and she was aware throughout that she was being watched and followed by secret police or foreign agents. I tried to hustle her away into the drawing room where I said I would of course look into the matter. She told me she would not leave until I had dismissed two members of my staff to whom she had already spoken and who, quite clearly, were also secret police shadowing her. I explained that they had both been teaching at the school for over ten years which surely was an over-elaborate under-cover occupation but she would have none of it. I nipped into my study next door to 'phone the police and when I returned she was back amongst the cricketers haranguing them once more on what a disgraceful school it was with the most extraordinary people masquerading as members of the teaching staff.

I took her by the arm to lead her away from the now enormously entertained cricketers when she said "take your hand off me or I shall have you on a charge or assault and battery." I was beginning to wonder how long this pantomime would continue when the police arrived and took her back to her car. There in the car was her handbag and in the ignition her car keys. In the boot was her picnic basket. The police then escorted her off the grounds and she was never heard of again.

Boarding schools are often used as neutral territory by parents who are separated or divorced. I was always very happy to provide the continuity of life at school where a boy knew the routine and was amongst friends when home life had been broken and the child was both insecure and vulnerable. Sometimes, however, I found myself being asked by one parent to stop the boy seeing the other parent for fear he would be kidnapped or taken abroad.

This was not an easy situation to resolve and it was fatal to take sides. When religion was also involved things became even more complicated and on one occasion I received a copy of a letter to a boy's father which was also copied to H E The Cardinal Archbishop of Westminster. I quote: 'I do not at this stage have any objection to the fact that Henry is being indoctrinated with two basic heresies, namely a blend of pantheism and Pelagianism. I have little doubt that the immediate appeal of these two errors will be removed logically as he gets older. However, they are both totally opposed to the orthodox creed.' I was not aware of indoctrinating any boy in any heresy, but it shows how difficult these situations could become.

Although goblins seemed to lurk round every corner and thwart one's plans and hopes they were not what I would

consider 'foul fiends' which, however, occasionally did appear. One such occasion was just what one hoped to avoid in that I found myself speaking on the 'phone to the father of a boy who was demanding access although I had been informed that any such access should be arranged through his estranged wife. The conversation took an unpleasant turn when he said: "Headmaster, I have many men working for me. It is easy for me to find out where you live." "Are you threatening me?" I asked. "I am not threatening you; I am warning you", came the reply. I had visions of my country cottage being set ablaze while I was stuck at the school unable to prevent it.

Talking of being set ablaze I treasured one Science report on a boy which said: "His amateur experiments in the art of pyrotechnics came well nigh setting the laboratory ablaze on more than one occasion."

Another unpleasant incident occurred when I was 'phoned by a parent at about ten o'clock one evening to say that he and his family had received a terrorist threat and that I was to keep a very close watch on his son, Oliver, as a kidnapping was a possibility. I was not to tell anyone including the teachers and, of course, not the boy for fear of alarming him. I rather wished I hadn't been told for fear of alarming me and asked whether the police would come round in the morning to advise me on what preventative action I should take. I was told that this was not a matter for the police but for the anti-terrorist squad. "Would they be coming round first thing in the morning?" I inquired. "No," came the reply, adding that they were too busy with the IRA in the run-up to Christmas, but had advised that the boy's best defence lay in anonymity amongst so many others. I knew full well that if any car drove in and asked the first boy for Oliver, as there was a parcel for him from his mother in the car, he would be produced in a flash.

At that time Oliver's dormitory was at my end of the building so that I knew that the terrorists would have to pass my quarters if they were planning to kidnap him at night, but I must say I fully expected the rhododendrons to erupt with balaclava-clad figures holding automatic weapons when I took the dogs out last thing that night. So I went to bed, but for the rest of that term the slightest sound at night had me leaping up to investigate to assure myself that all was well.

By day the most likely time for kidnapping Oliver was when the boys were outside in the mid-morning break, or during afternoon games. I usually went outside myself at these times anyway to exercise the dogs and watch the boys practising and playing games. On Sunday afternoons, however, they would play a variety of invented games which usually involved creeping through the undergrowth in the woods and then dashing across open spaces hoping not to be seen by the other side. The only thing to do, I concluded, was to follow Oliver, as if by chance, during these games and I soon became fighting fit with all the exertion, although the odd bit of bracken in my hair and scratch marks from brambles must have caused the staff to wonder what I was up to. Finally, when lack of sleep and too much exercise reduced me to exhaustion, I had to involve two or three members of the staff so that we could share the burden. The term ended and Christmas came and went, so, at the start of the next term I asked Oliver's father if the threat was now over. Oh, no, he said, the experts had told him that terrorists often wait till you have relaxed your guard.

CHAPTER FOUR

Oh happy servant he,
In such a posture found!
(No 229, *Hymns Ancient & Modern*)

I have described various postures or positions I found myself in when headmaster of a Prep school in the preceding pages. I remember on one occasion attending an headmasters' conference which was held annually over two or three days, usually at an Oxford or Cambridge college. When I took over as headmaster there was a boy in the school, named Giles, whose father was headmaster of another Prep school and an important figure at the conference. On the first night there was a drinks party so that we could mix and get to know each other and the hosts were the members of council of which Giles' father was one. Seeing me arrive and looking rather lost he kindly came up and said, "Hello, I should know who you are." "Yes," I couldn't resist replying, "you probably should. I'm your son's headmaster."

Members of one's staff from time to time found themselves in awkward postures. There was a retired Group Captain, known to the boys as Groupie (luckily not gropey), whose teaching career with us had to cease fairly soon after his voice was heard above the general hubbub coming from his classroom saying in pleading tones, "Please be decent; I'm decent, why can't you be decent?" We also had a Major who could be found on occasion standing on his head in the staff common room. The common room was often very crowded and there was a large table in the centre. When the Major wished to cross the room he often chose the easiest way and crawled under the table. On one occasion I was at a dinner party he gave and he sat at the end of the table in a tight corner from which he could not get out. Remembering that he had forgotten something just as his guests had sat down, he dived under the table and emerged at the other end. I was quite used to this and carried on talking to my neighbour, but some of the other guests were rendered speechless for most of the meal.

Parents would often ask to see me to discuss their son's future schooling and academic progress. Most kept to the point and did not delay, as I usually had other parents waiting for similar discussions. One evening I had spent an hour with a boy's parents going over and over again the same points until I began to understand why the boy's academic progress was so slow. Eventually the Dame decided to rescue me and popped her head round the door to say that Mr and Mrs So-and-So were over from the Continent and would like a brief word.

Seeing my chance I leapt up, but so did the parents I was with as they exclaimed, "Oh! Just the people we want to see to arrange that our sons meet in the holidays." Horror registered on the Dame's face who then told me in a whisper that she was only trying to rescue me and that Mr and Mrs So-and-So were not even in the country. That took some explaining away.

Often when I found myself in an awkward position it was entirely my fault because I had told some small white lie so as not to hurt someone's feelings or so as to save them embarrassment. A small lie often then has to be supported by a bigger one and the situation can soon get quite out of control. Let me give you an example. When I was up at Cambridge gowns had to be worn for all lectures, supervisions and meals in hall as well as after dark. Undergraduates often picked up the first gown they saw whether it was the correct one or not (College gowns differed in various details). The same 'borrowing' happened with bicycles so it was essential to secure your bicycle with a padlock and chain. But the most coveted item of all was a bicycle pump and on one occasion I inadvertently 'stole' one. I shall explain.

Trinity had a large underground bicycle store with possibly as many as 200 places for bicycles. One morning I went down to collect my bicycle only to discover that the back tyre was flat. I looked around, but was sure that no one would have left a pump on his bicycle, when suddenly I saw a beautiful, shining, new bicycle, obviously lovingly polished and equipped with all the latest gadgets including a pump. I borrowed it. Just as I had finished pumping up my back tyre I turned to replace it on the gleaming model near by. Then I saw him. He was quite clearly the proud owner striding along among the rusty old machines towards his pride and joy. I knew at once that he would suspect me of attempting to steal his pump if I returned it to him. It was as though I had been caught red-handed. I did what, no sooner than done, turned out to be a mistake. I slid the pump up the sleeve of my sports-coat. I then had to lock up my bicycle (pretending that I had just arrived and parked it) and make my way towards the stairs leading up from the bicycle store.

I don't know whether you've ever had that nasty feeling (normally when acting in a school production) of wondering which arm swings with which leg and which way as you walk on to the stage. Well, try walking normally with a bicycle pump up your sleeve and, worse, try going upstairs. I stumbled several times but made it to the top and then set out across Great Court to my rooms. I was certain that the owner, suspicion aroused, was following me. I walked faster but didn't look round. Finally I came to my staircase and was up a couple of flights in a flash falling only twice. I shot into my room, closed the door, put the pump down my bed and collapsed into a chair pretending to be idly reading the newspaper.

When I thought it was safe to emerge, I set out for the bicycle store with the pump up my sleeve in order to return it. But the bicycle was not there. Back to my room I went to find a more sensible place to conceal the pump until I could marry it up with its matching bicycle. Life thereafter is a blur in my memory of constant sorties in daylight, after dark, taking different routes so as not to be spotted and thought to be acting suspiciously, but always failing to find the elusive bicycle so that I could complete my clandestine errand and replace the pump which I was now quite used to having residing up my sleeve. Eventually, after what seemed like many weeks and hundreds of miles of toing and froing with a furtive look (sometimes in dark glasses) and a stiff arm, the dread work was accomplished and I had got away with it without any embarrassment to either party. It was several more weeks, however, before I remembered how to walk naturally and swing both arms freely without let or hindrance.

I can recollect two incidents when boys found themselves in awkward positions. The first concerns the French Oral examination which had just been introduced and consequently was the cause of much fear, particularly amongst the less able linguists (who were, of course, the vast majority). The entire oral interview was tape recorded and the poor boy would have an overwhelming sensation of impending doom as the master asking the questions pressed the button to record. On this occasion Richard, the boy being interviewed and who was unlikely to grow up to follow a career as an interpreter in any language including his own, but who in every other way was a delightful boy, was white with fear. The master started with an easy question: "Quel âge avez-vous?" There was a long silence and some swallowing sounds and then Richard's voice can be heard: "Je suis ... J'ai ... Je ... Oh Christ."

The other incident concerns a boy named William and his ex-fighter pilot but now elderly Mathematics teacher who used to expectorate plentifully while explaining about the square on the hypotenuse (particularly on "hypotenuse") covering the front row of desks in a fine spray. William, I believe in all innocence, asked the master: "Sir, how many Messerschmitts did you shoot down with your Spit?" William was a fair-haired boy with a pale complexion, but realizing what he had said, is rumoured to have turned a shade which can best be described as a mixture between vermilion and puce.

I am sure the boy blushed in the following incident which occurred in a Latin lesson. It was the custom when memorising Latin verbs to sit the boys on benches and move them up the order if they could answer a question or continue a conjugation when several of the boys higher than them had failed. The boys enjoyed the competition and it made for a lively lesson. On this occasion, however, a boy had lost concentration and his thoughts were miles away when the master said to him "On you go, Hutchins." Hutchins, waking up with a start, hastily launched into: "Onugo, Onugis, Onugit".

CHAPTER FIVE

Could we but climb where Moses stood,
and view the landscape o'er

(No 285, *Hymns Ancient & Modern*)

I have mentioned 'prospective' parents in an earlier chapter. I once received a 'phone call to say that the wife of a Middle-Eastern king wished to visit the school with her son. On the appointed day they duly arrived in a chauffeur-driven car, followed by another car out of which leapt some sinister-looking men who fanned out around the grounds and garden surrounding the private side. I welcomed her into the drawing room and just as we were exchanging pleasantries the Dame's large Afghan hound bounced into the room and pranced towards the boy, clearly intent on engaging in a wrestling match with him. His mother leapt up to intervene, explaining that the boy was allergic to dogs and I managed to bundle the dog out of the room, but not before it had put both paws on my shoulders and given me the friendliest of greetings. Just as order was being restored and we were picking up where we had left off, the garden door burst open and in came my two yellow Labradors. We carried on with the discussion, when peace was restored, and then had a look round the school, but I could tell that it was not going to be the right school for the boy.

Another time I was informed that a Royal Duke and Duchess wanted to visit. I think the month was February because rain and dead leaves were travelling horizontally across the windows of the drawing room and upstairs there were 90 boys in bed with 'flu. They duly arrived, nearly an hour late, and the Duchess was horrified to hear that we had boys ill with 'flu as in her words: "The Duke must not catch it as he is going on an official visit to

the Middle East early next week". We therefore confined our tour to those parts of the school where boys who had not got 'flu were engaged in various activities, as games outside were not possible in the appalling weather. Most of the surviving boys were in some hobbies rooms and this meant battling across a courtyard with the rain stinging one's face.

Our dishevelled party arrived in the model-making room, but no one took much notice as I had not told anyone (including staff) who I was showing round that day in the belief that the Duke and Duchess would much rather see things as they are and not have a special performance put on for them. The most intelligent boy in the school at the time, named Nicholas, was busily constructing a three-masted ship which was quite well advanced. I leant over his shoulder and said, "What's that you're making?" Nicholas clearly thought it was a very silly question (which it was, but one has to say something on these extended tours round the school), but he managed a moderately polite reply:

"It's a ship, Sir," he said, scarcely looking up.

"And are you going to paint it?" said the Duke, trying to jolly things along. One silly question Nicholas could just about cope with but two was asking too much.

"Yup," he said, without looking up.

When I was first teaching at the school Prince Charles came over to play in an under-eleven cricket match. In those days security was less of a concern and the detective that came with the visiting team spent the warm afternoon asleep in the school bus. Prince William also came on several occasions and on one of these Princess Diana also came to watch him playing football. I thought I would not interrupt her by introducing myself and left her to watch the match in peace, chatting to a friend who had come with her. After matches one always provided tea in the drawing room for all the parents who had come to watch, and when I got back to the private side I found the drawing room full of expectant (if you get my meaning) mothers hoping to meet the princess.

"Well, is she coming?" they chorused.

"I haven't asked her," I replied.

"Why ever not?" came the disappointed cry.

"Well," I said, "she couldn't possibly come in here as she was wearing trousers." The newspapers next day came close to having the headline: 'Headmaster lynched by mob of maddened mothers.'

In my time as headmaster mothers took over the running of their sons' Prep school education and they liked to intervene on their sons' behalf whenever they thought it would help, which was often. One mother 'phoned me to say that her son had just been on the 'phone in tears because he was not selected for the under-eleven cricket team. I explained that he had been in the under-eleven football team so perhaps cricket gave a chance to another boy to represent the school.

"Headmaster, do you realize that you are totally destroying my son's morale?" came the answer. I explained that that was not the intention and that in any case I did not select the team. I was told that in future I should select teams on the basis of a rota so that everyone could have a turn and then no one would be disappointed.

Most mothers, however, soon understood how the system worked and left things to the school to handle. Sometimes they expected the school to perform all sorts of tasks to cure a variety of ills. I quote from one letter. 'We are most concerned at John's round shoulders – can he have remedial exercises or something please? Richard's twitchy eye is very bad – any ideas on that? John has a tooth coming through the roof of his mouth. The dentist wants to take this out soon. I will ring you next week to discuss it with you. Best wishes for the term. P S, Richard says please can he not have rice pudding as it makes him feel sick.'

One mother, who lived in France, was always very concerned that her son Johnny should not travel without his anorak. She would always ring the school to remind us to check that Johnny was wearing his anorak when he went on half-term exeats or weekends with friends. I would leave notes around the private side to remind me to check that Johnny had his anorak.

At the end of term some boys would be taken by bus to the local station to catch the train to London. I would read out the 'train list' at breakfast and those boys would go out of the room first, the majority following later as they were going to be collected by car. A few boys would have taxis booked to take them to airports. What with flights departing from different airports and different terminals at different times it all took a lot of organizing which was done by the school secretary. At the end of one term Johnny was due to fly from Heathrow to France, but in the general chaos at the end of term his mother failed to get through to me with instructions about his anorak, so, quite late at night, she telephoned the staff common room. Her call was taken by a young member of staff.

When I read out the 'train list' at breakfast the young master rushed up to say that Johnny's mother had told him specifically to make sure Johnny wore his anorak when he went on the train next day. It was early in the morning and the secretary had not yet arrived. I thought there had been a mistake and Johnny's name should have been on the train list, so I told him to hurry up and jump on the bus before it departed. I thought the crisis was over, but in fact it was only just beginning.

The secretary arrived and explained that Johnny was going by taxi to Heathrow and that she had his air ticket and passport to give him. A frantic 'phone call to the local station revealed that the train for London had just left. Johnny was on it. Somebody then appeared saying that he had found Johnny's anorak in his classroom. Johnny's taxi then arrived. The taxi driver was given the ticket, passport and anorak and told to drive like the son of Jehu to Reading station to collect Johnny and take him to Heathrow. An emergency call was put through to Reading station to get Johnny off the train. Shortly afterwards the train pulled into Reading with one carriage occupied by about 30 highly excited boys and a couple of harassed members of staff.

There was an announcement made over the station loudspeaker system, which, by the grace of God and a stroke of unparalleled luck, one of the masters heard. Johnny was bundled off the train, unaware that a monumental drama was unfolding in which he was the leading character, and he waited patiently until the taxi arrived and picked him up, united him with his anorak, air ticket and passport together with luggage which mercifully, had not been put in the bus for the station as it was amongst the luggage lined up for the taxis. The crisis therefore had a happy ending and I believe, to this day, that Johnny's mother never knew what chaos her late night 'phone call had caused.

One year about a dozen of our best cricketers and three members of staff went on a cricket tour to Barbados. There they were to play six matches and spend some days watching the Test match that was to take place in Barbados between Australia and the West Indies. A number of parents decided to go too and booked into one hotel while the boys and staff in charge booked into a less expensive hotel. I was able to keep in touch by sending fax messages to the parents' hotel which they would receive over breakfast, and then they would fax me in the evening with the results of the latest match, which I would find waiting for me the following morning.

One boy named George, who had a particularly sunny disposition, sent me a postcard which he got all the boys to sign picturing three lovely topless girls viewed from behind. He wrote: 'having great fun out here – we've seen lots of girls like this facing in the other direction!' I immediately sent off a fax to one of the mothers saying that I was delighted with the boys' postcard and would she please ask them to send me lots more. I don't think she understood why, on passing on my message to the boys, she was greeted with much giggling.

CHAPTER SIX

In wisdom let us grow,
As years and strength are given

(No 338, *Hymns Ancient & Modern*)

The mention of cricket brings one particular story to mind of an under-eleven team playing a match at another school. Only one master could be spared to accompany them and so he had to act as an umpire throughout the game. When his side was fielding it would be easy enough as he could give whispered instructions to his captain about bowling changes and field placings. When batting however, he would be stuck in the middle and so the captain would have to make his own decisions about which batsman should go in next and so on.

On this particular occasion they arrived by bus, lost the toss, and were put in to bat (an old ploy hoping to get the visitors out while they were still feeling ill after the journey). The young ten-year-old captain asked his cricket master when he should declare and the master replied "When I drop my shooting stick." At the end of the third over with the score on 11, the master stumbled as he walked in from his position at square leg and, in trying to save himself from falling, dropped his shooting stick. His young captain eager to please immediately declared his side's innings over. Under-eleven cricket is totally unpredictable and full of surprises and on this occasion the declaration proved sound as the other side was all out for nine.

In an earlier chapter I mentioned the annual golf holiday at the Royal St David's course on the west coast of Wales. Some of the party were very good golfers and some were decidedly not of which I was one. I had only started to play when I began teaching as the school possessed a small course. The boys, who started at a young age, had natural swings and could not see that it was a difficult game at all, but although the clubs that I acquired were called Truswing (a sobriquet that I was known by on our golf holidays), the truth was that my swing had various kinks and loops of varying numbers each time I played a shot, with unpredictable, or rather all too predictable, results. Thankfully the other members of the party were there to enjoy themselves and my presence added considerably to their level of enjoyment.

Fortunately I was not the only erratic golfer in the group and another member of staff provided an equal amount of fun. He had the loudest and most infectious laugh I have ever heard so one could always tell where he was amongst the sand dunes on the course. Once my attention was drawn by peals of laughter blown down by the biting wind and I saw a windmill action taking place in a bunker. He had gone in on three and came out on thirteen. On another occasion I was partnering him in foursomes and it was his turn to drive on the elevated eleventh tee. I saw trouble looming as he rose up on to his toes high on his backswing and the ball, when struck, made a loud whirring noise as it shot off towards midwicket. There was then a sharp crack as it hit a wooden fencing post after which it disappeared towards backward short-leg relative to our position on the tee. This was followed by a short, eerie silence and then a metallic ping as the ball struck the flag pole on the previous green which we had just vacated.

I was once playing with the parent of a boy on the course at Piltdown in Sussex. I was much encouraged to be told that the course had no bunkers, but as events turned out it didn't need any. I looked across at my opponent on one hole and saw him standing in deep rough. He then played what looked like a series of shots while I counted away merrily. "What ever happened?" I asked as my exhausted opponent returned to the fairway, thinking that this was one hole that I might win. "I was killing a snake," he replied.

As I have said the boys seemed to find the game easy and once when I was fairly new on the staff, I was playing with a boy named Johnny. He was a good athlete and in various teams. As we were playing one hole the junior form mistress drove past behind a line of trees. Foolishly I said, "I bet you can't hit her car." Before I could stop him Johnny dropped a ball on the ground and, with a lazy swing, propelled it over the intervening brick fives courts so that it disappeared from our view. A loud clanging noise told me that he had won the bet.

In those far off days all the old traditions of behaviour in the schoolboy code still existed and one of the taboos was swanking. It was customary to precede or follow a remark, which might be considered boasting by other boys, with the words 'non-swank'. On the golf course before a boy played his shot from the tee he would warn the players in front by shouting: "Fore! If I get as far." This saved him from the charge of swanking about how far he hit the ball.

In those distant days there was a retired Colonel on the staff who dressed smartly and who had a good sense of humour. Somewhat incongruously, as he was a large man, he would arrive each morning in a bubble car, but would step out in a well-tailored tweed coat often sporting a flower in his buttonhole and always wearing a highly polished pair of hand made brown leather shoes. The Colonel had served in the Far East during the war and, if one asked him where he got his shoes he would reply, "I took them off a dead man in Jakarta."

Over the years some fairly extraordinary people were employed in one capacity or another and I remember in particular one nursing sister. Her rooms were above the dining room and looked out over the playing fields to one of the other houses where the staff kept a barrel of beer in the cellar and had a small bar. The younger men on the staff would gather there at about eight o'clock in the evening for some drinks before dinner.

Dinner, in fact, was placed in a hot plate at seven o'clock in the boys' dining room with one table laid for staff to come when it suited them. This was a convenient arrangement although it meant that things were rather dried up by nine or even ten when one arrived to eat. The nursing sister in question could observe our arrival from upstairs and would then come down to dinner. We would suddenly hear a rustling noise and she would come shimmering in dressed in a full length black chiffon dress and smothered in scent.

This became a nightly hazard and in the winter when the evenings were dark we would come over without using our torches to escape detection. As soon as the dining room lights were turned on, however, she would spot it from upstairs and within seconds the apparition had joined us for dinner. One night I suggested we took a candle with us to light the table for dinner and thus escape being noticed. The plan was working well until, in the semi-darkness, one of our group dropped the metal vegetable dish. The noise caused an immediate manifestation of the apparition and we had some difficulty explaining the candle which, we said, was in connection with the possibility of a power cut.

This was not so far-fetched as it sounds as power cuts were a frequent occurrence. The power lines came overhead through the woods and it took only a minor gale to bring a branch down across the cable plunging us all into darkness. This was always welcomed by the boys, particularly if it happened during prep in the evening. In the three-day week in the 1970s there were power cuts of three hours duration, but the local paper published when these would occur and one could alter the timetable accordingly. The boys were far from delighted to find that prep could take place after lunch if a cut was scheduled for the evening. However one still had to occupy them and so on those occasions the staff would provide an entertainment lit by a couple of gas lights and some candles. Occasionally I found myself shaving at midnight before going to bed as the next cut was scheduled for when one woke in the morning.

The great storm of 1987 partially missed us and did far less damage than the storm on Thursday, 25th January 1990. This storm brought down 40 trees on the school property alone and we were without power for five days. Our neighbouring schools closed and sent the boys home but we were determined not to be defeated. We had one generator which meant that the main school boiler could operate. This meant that we had heating in the classrooms and hot water for showers after games. Cooking was done by Calor gas so we could have hot meals. There was no light anywhere after dark and no heat in the other houses occupied by boys and staff and of course in the private side. Being denied my daily bath started to tell on my morale until I hit on the plan of setting off at about 11 o'clock at night with a torch to have a shower in the shower room adjoining the boys' changing room. It was a largish tiled room which was fairly cold at that hour, but there were ten showers to choose from and the water was hot.

At the end of the Christmas term there would be a school concert on Saturday and Sunday in the afternoon and parents would choose which day they wanted to come. The concert was followed by tea and then the parents would look round a variety of exhibitions which the boys laid on proudly, showing what they had accomplished during the term in art, or model-making, or whichever of the many activities they enjoyed. At the end of the Easter term there was the school play which was always very ambitious involving a cast of up to 60 boys. The stage was in the Sports Hall and was very well equipped with flood lights, spot lights and electrical devices and the whole hall was heated by under floor heating.

Several weeks before these events invitations would be sent

out to all the parents and friends of the school and they would reply on postcards provided stipulating which day they would like to come and how large their party would be. One then had an idea what size the audience would be for each performance and how many thousands of sandwiches and so on would be needed.

One year the invitations had all gone out for the school play and replies were coming in steadily when the Southern Electricity Board sent us a letter saying that major work had to be carried out and there would be no power for 12 hours, from eight o'clock in the morning of the Saturday when the play was scheduled. The bursar was asked to contact the SEB at once and insist that they provide us with generators 'sufficient in size to power the QE2.' This they were reluctant to do, but after much palaver they agreed.

On the Friday evening before the Saturday of the play performance two large lorries arrived each with a generator about the size of a caravan. These were unloaded and at eight o'clock next morning they were started up. They made a huge noise and caused everything to vibrate within 50 yards, but the play duly went ahead and all was well. At about five o'clock as the parents were thinking of going home the lights throughout the school began to flicker and grow dimmer until they gradually faded away altogether. The generators had run out of petrol, but the crisis had been averted and the play had gone ahead successfully, so we felt well pleased with our success.

CHAPTER SEVEN

The lot is fallen unto me in a fair ground:
Yea I have a goodly heritage
(Psalm 16)

I mentioned in the previous chapter that parents could stipulate how many seats they required for school plays or concerts. The Sports Hall could seat well over 300 and with two performances there was plenty of room for all. This meant that granny could come as well as nanny and they guaranteed an appreciative audience.

One granny, whose husband had not been well after an accident, came with her husband to the school concert and then wrote a letter of thanks. However, the letter became mislaid and when discovered three months later she sent it to me with a second letter explaining what had happened. I quote both letters verbatim:

5th December 1983

Dear Headmaster

'If music be the food of love, play on.' You will have to carve that on the inspirational music stands. And indeed how marvellous it would be if still we could hearken to the straining harmonies so recently caressing the willing ear. (I think I mean harmonious strains, sorry Boys.)

It is just wonderful to live all over again the singular privilege that it was to witness the dedication and the enthusiastic effort on the part of so many within the staging of such an accomplished and memorable Concert. We had a lovely time. It was a great celebration for us along the somewhat craggy Pilgrim's Way thus to enshrine for all time the astonishing, the

near miraculous, and now progressive recovery of my
Husband from that annihilating accident.

I honestly think he has been to the gates of hell and back, my
far less worthy self meanwhile fortified by the consoling
reflection that the Good are never totally consigned. As for the
Bad, we know not. But, resiliently optimistic, I am hoping he
will instruct me in the shooting of the rapids towards the
Higher Reaches. And before I am confounded by some
learned Gentleman such as your esteemed Self, may I make it
clear that my River Styx is going to flow backwards and no
arguing. Not even with your distinguished Geography Master.

But some people in this not usually so dusty vale of tears do
have to endure, and what a fine trumpeting day it was to mark
his recovery. Nothing could have registered in this context in
manner quite so telling as your kind invitation (all right then,
your kind acquiescence!) to us to appear on that reverberating
occasion.

Gosh, how the Choir sang, perfectly timed and responsive and
disciplined. This last factor perhaps the most telling in the
discomposed world of today, and an all time echoing memory
of an endeavour so well submitted and presented with a
marvellous kind of fluid flow as one performance succeeded
another. The background of music to something special is
most certainly something that a Young Person will remember
in advancing years upon a sort of ineradicable implant. Like a
haunting nostalgic scent, or the elusive familiarity of some
outline as you round a corner and know without reason that
you have travelled that way before. And most of all when
music, the most yearning phenomenal presentation of all,
summarily recalls the joy of times long gone. Handkerchiefs
please!

I was proud to be there and even so far forgot myself as
inadvertently to join in the bits of Rule Britannia where I

should have maintained a restrained silence, having by some oversight failed to read the explicit instruction relating thereto. Though I think my gritty growling key did not sustain against the general perfection of pitch. But, within a context that we all can recognize if not too relevant coming from me, having started you have to finish - however quacky upon realisation the last faint ebbing stanza.

We did not complete our tour of the Classrooms due to Grandfather's inability to sustain the familiar upright stance for very long. You will be relieved to hear therefore that I did not have opportunity to pinch any magazine pre-views, which once upon a time to my great mortification I mistook for souvenir take-aways, and within all conscience had to return the interesting contents of my shaming pockets upon discovery of this lamentable looting.

The years roll on, as old folks such as myself do not have to be reminded, and such golden moments as your Concert do not readily vouchsafe again. But such sustained spell of octave upon arpeggio loftily may ascend us to the Spheres momentarily to keep company with the 'Quiring Cherubims.' Where, according to Raphael, no less, lumpy outlines (such as mine own but whisper it) are regularly permitted to grace the scene.

As we carved passage through the darkness on the fairly long haul home, I heard again the echo of a great afternoon, and was irresistibly reminded that

' We are less than a spark of His fire,
Or a moment's mood of His Soul.
We are lost in the notes on the lips of His Choir
That chant the chant of the whole.'

7th March 1984

Dear Headmaster

I am sick to the soul, as you may imagine, to discover that this letter which I dare not open lest it be stuffed more than usually full of my usual rubbish has never been posted. It has been discovered behind a large lump of furniture in the hall, having slid from the mail heap, and is a sorry reflection indeed upon how rarely things get moved for cleaning behind in this house. Actually it is an even greater total mortification because I have long argued with the Insurance about delivery of a certain rather vital communication, also now discovered within the sorry scattering. But regarding that Outfit I refuse to wear my Dunce's hat down to my collar, unless I can brush aside the main balance of ashes on my head permitting some view out of the top. But to you, unequivocally my humble addresses freely are presented. I just have to hope that matters of import like our pleasure in your Concert lose nothing by delay. A somewhat fatuous comment that I will not emphasize lest I invite some deserved shrapnel such as a succinct admonition to seek the origin of the word 'naïve'.

I am truly truly sorry. And now you are caught for a further appearance this week-end.

Thank you for making it possible for us to come. Anywhere will do against the back wall, or in the corridor. I can recognize the pressures and claims and thank you in advance for your kind welcome (forbearance, God bless it) to yet another illustrious occasion.

It is a lovely day down here. It makes you want to climb the trees and set up a house agency for the birds. They are bickering quite dreadfully around the place for favourite nesting sites. And yet next week within our capricious weather, the Big Sillies could be twigged to a frozen bough.

But not to worry since hope is all and Birdsong comes next. For that all the world is listening.

Yours ...

When I returned after Cambridge to become a permanent member of the staff in 1962 I was given a room in what was colloquially known as Muck Cottage. In my last year at Trinity I had occupied rooms in a new building which was centrally heated day and night, whether you liked it or not; Muck Cottage had no heating and we were just starting the winter of 1962/63 which together with 1947 is the worst in my memory. When the winter closed in the whole drive on the slope by the Wellingtonia became a sheet of ice and in order to be warm enough to sleep in bed I had to wear a vest, cricket sweater and dressing gown as well as pyjamas and a thick woolly pair of socks.

Muck Cottage was occupied by the night watchman called Fred. He had started work as boot boy in 1889 and had retired in 1934 to take on the job of night watchman. This involved coming up to the main school building at about ten o'clock at night. He would then make a large pot of tea to take to the common room, where there would be several members of staff marking books. Fred revelled in telling stories which one could prompt him to do very easily and they were always word perfect.

One day when he was a young man, Fred met the headmaster's wife in the corridor: "Fred," she said, "we'll have to discharge you."

"Yes, Ma'am," he said. Later that day he met the headmaster: "Fred," he said, "we'll build you a cottage," and he did too. It was named Muck Cottage because it was near the school's own recently built sewage works and I suspect the plan was to make Fred keep an eye on things to make sure it was working properly.

The school cook in those far off days was called Mrs Bussell. She used to get up at about five o'clock in the morning in order to cook breakfast for the whole school, but was unable to face the day's work until she had had two pints of beer. One day:

"The headmaster had a case of whisky sent up from Harveys of Bristol; after he had unpacked it Mrs Bussell said, 'tidy up them straws, Fred.' I was feeling in the box and there was a whole bottle left behind. 'Look Mrs Bussell.' I said and blimey! she snatched it out of my hand. That was the last I saw of it. But I got my own back. Sometime later she asked me to buy her a bottle of whisky and gave me 3s 6d. That's what whisky cost them days. A couple of days later she said, 'Did I ever pay you for that bottle of whisky, Fred?' 'No, Mrs Bussell,'" I said.

Fred continued as night watchman until over the age of 90. Another old retainer was Bill Smith. His father had been the school founder's coachman and Bill took over from him and served the school for 50 years with the rather grander title of chauffeur. He was always known as 'Smith' and this caused a junior mistress much embarrassment when she was gossiping one day and brought out the phrase: "When I was bathing Smith," to which a senior member of staff said "Smith the boy or Smith the chauffeur?"

Smith had some wonderfully muddled expressions he used to produce of which I remember a few: "He's not the only fly in the woodpile" and "That puts a completely different kettle on it." I was particularly delighted when he came out with the exquisite malapropism: "I don't want to be casting nasturtiums on him".

During my time as headmaster I was occasionally invited by a parent or Old Boy of the school to some occasion which was particularly memorable. One of these occurred when the Commander-in-Chief Naval Home Command, an Old Boy, invited me to dinner on board HMS Victory. I drove down to

❤

Admiralty House, Portsmouth and on arrival handed over my car keys. I went in and met the Admiral and was then taken upstairs to my room. There I found my suitcase had been unpacked and my dinner jacket was hanging up. Poured out for me was a gin and tonic. After bathing and dressing I went down for a pre-dinner drink with the other guests.

"You had better come in my car" the Admiral then said, and we drove around to the Victory. He told me, "I had better go on board first" which was just as well because as I followed him up we were piped aboard. We then went into the ship and came to a grand staircase that led to Nelson's quarters. Suddenly a trumpet fanfare was sounded as we went up the staircase. There were about a dozen guests for dinner each with a sailor standing behind his or her chair ready to serve and remove plates. After dinner we were taken on a tour of the ship, which was quite an experience in itself, and then back to Admiralty House for a brandy before bed. When the time to go came after breakfast next morning I found my case was packed and in the car, the car was outside the door with the key in the ignition and a newspaper was on the passenger seat. The Royal Navy certainly knows how to look after its guests.

One of our seven scholarship candidates another year was a godson of the Cabinet Secretary and he arranged for me to bring up all seven boys to London and look round 10 Downing Street.

Mrs Thatcher was Prime Minister at the time but was away in Scotland, otherwise our visit would not have been possible. I drove down Whitehall with a car load of boys and put on my indicator to turn into Downing Street. The police checked up on us and then let us through. Security is a great deal stricter now, but we enjoyed ourselves sitting round the Cabinet Table and had our photograph taken outside the door of No 10 by the policeman on duty.

Another time the godfather to one of our scholarship candidates was the Chief Secretary to the Treasury, who also happened to be my cousin. He arranged for us to look round the Houses of Parliament and we had our sandwich lunch in his room in what, in those days, were known as 'the corridors of power'. A third visit to both the Houses of Parliament and 10 Downing Street was arranged for all the boys who were leaving the school in my last term as headmaster. Two boys who had got scholarships that year (a major one to Radley and the top scholarship to Eton) were both the sons of MPs who kindly took us round everywhere and explained everything to the boys and on this occasion we had lunch on the terrace overlooking the Thames.

One parent, who owned a Tiger Moth, very kindly invited me and two others on the staff up for a flight. We drove to a grassy field some miles away and took it in turns for a 20-minute flight over the school and back. While waiting our turn to go up we were given delicious smoked salmon sandwiches and large gin and tonics. One had to take care in climbing aboard the Tiger Moth not to put one's foot through the wing and we wore a Biggles-style leather helmet so that the pilot could speak to us through ear phones. I had planned to drop a weighted parcel over the side which would contain instructions for prep for my mathematics form, but the plan was abandoned because of the danger of damaging the tail plane.

Throughout my time as headmaster I managed to avoid expelling any boy, although on several occasions I sent boys home so that they could cool down and reassess what they were trying to achieve at school. This also gave me a chance to calm down, which was sometimes just as necessary. I always enjoyed the comment of one headmaster to the parents of a boy he wanted to have removed from his school: "He would do better at either a smaller or a larger school."

I am sure every boy could tell a story of a lucky escape or some escapade which nearly went wrong and many stories, no doubt, would dwell on the eccentricities of their teachers. A typical example is of the public school boy who rounded a corner in the town near to his school while smoking a cigarette and bumped straight into a member of staff. "Jesus," he said, and the master replied, "Yes, but strictly incognito," before walking on.

It must have made it all worth while.

And with the morn those angel faces smile
Which I have loved long since, and lost a while.

(No 298, *Hymns Ancient & Modern*)